MORE than Your Mountains

What Readers are Saying ...

Author Whitney Ward has drawn from her personal journey battling a chronic illness for much of her life to create a God-inspired, inspirational message for children who face similar health challenges: God loves you and He hasn't abandoned you, and you are much more important to God than your illness.

The vibrant and imaginative illustrations by Courtney Smith bring Whitney's words to life. What child doesn't want to feel like a super hero or a swashbuckling pirate, especially on the roughest days of their illness?

While this book is written for children, parents and healthcare providers will also derive inspiration from Whitney's words. Young people often hear from adults that they are more than just the situation in which they find themselves. This book will serve to get this important message across to children in a way they can understand.
—**Dr. Randal Olshefski**, Section Chief of the Hematology and Oncology Department at Nationwide Children's Hospital and has been the author's specialist for twenty-two years.

As a parent of a child with medical conditions, I am thrilled to get to use this book as a tool to help ease those anxieties for her.
—**Heather McCutcheon**, Clinical Radiology Facilitator and lupus warrior who cheers her daughter through her own medical conditions.

MORE than Your Mountains

Whitney Lane Ward
illustrated by Courtney Smith

Copyright Notice
MORE Than Your Mountains
First edition. Copyright © 2021 by Whitney Lane Ward. The information contained in this book is the intellectual property of Whitney Lane Ward and is governed by United States and International copyright laws. All rights reserved. No part of this publication, either text or image, may be used for any purpose other than personal use. Therefore, reproduction, modification, storage in a retrieval system, or retransmission, in any form or by any means, electronic, mechanical, or otherwise, for reasons other than personal use, except for brief quotations for reviews or articles and promotions, is strictly prohibited without prior written permission by the publisher.

Scripture verses quoted come from the King James Version of the Bible. Public domain.

Cover and Interior Design: Courtney Smith, Derinda Babcock
Editor(s): Derinda Babcock, Deb Haggerty
Author Represented By: Cyle Young Literary Elite

PUBLISHED BY: Elk Lake Publishing, Inc., 35 Dogwood Drive, Plymouth, MA 02360, 2021

Library Cataloging Data
Names: Ward, Whitney Lane (Whitney Lane Ward)
MORE Than Your Mountains / Whitney Lane Ward
36 p. 21.6 cm × 21.6 cm (8.5 in × 8.5 in.)
ISBN-13: 978-1-64949-333-0 (paperback) | 978-1-64949-334-7 (trade hardcover) | 978-1-64949-335-4 (trade paperback) | 978-1-64949-336-1 (e-book)
Key Words: Chronic illness; children's illness; children's values; emotions & feelings; hospitals, doctors, nurses; overcoming challenges; cancer in kids
Library of Congress Control Number: 2021944462 Nonfiction

Author's Dedication

To all the children who are patients at Nationwide Children's Hospital and all the children in the world who bravely fight their illness—I see you.
You are victorious and you are MORE!

Illustrator's Dedication

To Titus, the fiercest dragon I know.

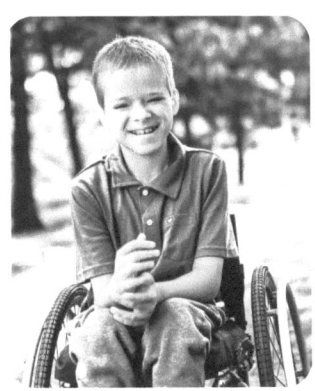

Did you know God made you MORE than your disease?

You are MORE than the
hair loss
that makes you feel old.

You are MORE than the kids who, at times, say mean things.

You are MORE than each bruise
and embarrassing scar.
You are MORE than all that—
you're a bright shooting star.

You were given this story, now, this is your time.

Do not be discouraged.

Say,

"I WILL NOT FEAR!"

Shout this powerful message
for all people to hear.

Your disease didn't beat you.
It just made you tough.
God made you and said,
"Child, you're MORE than enough!"

Comforting Scripture Verses

Fear thou not; for I am with thee: be not dismayed; for I am thy God: I will strengthen thee; yea, I will help thee; yea, I will uphold thee with the right hand of my righteousness. Isaiah 41: 10 (KJV)

But they that wait upon the LORD shall renew their strength; they shall mount up with wings as eagles; they shall run, and not be weary; and they shall walk, and not faint. Isaiah 40:31

Trust in the LORD with all thine heart; and lean not unto thine own understanding. In all thy ways acknowledge him, and he shall direct thy paths. Proverbs 3:5-6

Author's Note

Spoons/spoonie theory: This concept was created by Christine Miserandino. It's a metaphor to visualize how much physical and mental energy a person with chronic illness has for the day. A sick person might think, "Okay, how many spoons do I have today?" And we refer to ourselves as spoonies.

Zebras: In medical school, med students are taught when you hear hoofbeats, think horses, not zebras. This means the most obvious diagnosis is usually the right one. But for patients who wait years to be diagnosed, patients who are still undiagnosed, or patients like me who have a rare disease, we are called zebras because our diagnosis wasn't obvious.

Bells: In pediatric hematology units, there's a bell. Even if you aren't a patient who has cancer, you know what the bell is for. Chemo is a hard, painful, and traumatic process. Doctors and nurses want their cancer patients to have something to look forward to once they are done with chemo and to celebrate how hard they fought. So on their last day of chemo, after they have finished, the child's family, doctors, and nurses gather around the child and celebrate and cheer as the child rings the bell with all their might. The excitement, strength, perseverance, and determination in those children's faces is truly an inspiring and heartwarming sight to behold!

Support/Encouragement Dogs: Many pediatric hospitals have support/encouragement dogs, typically golden retrievers, for children who have been in the hospital for a really long time or are facing a really scary procedure.

Interaction with a gentle and loving dog can ease the child's fears and anxiety, taking their mind off the mountain they are facing.

Hospital Bracelets for stuffed animals: When I was a young child, I underwent many surgeries. This process was always a little terrifying to me, especially when I was separated from my parents to be taken to the OR. The children's hospital where I had surgeries had a wonderful tradition of putting a hospital bracelet on the child's stuffed animal. *Lion King* was my favorite movie as a child, and I had a stuffed Simba that went to surgery with me. With my Simba laying beside me wearing the same hospital bracelet, I felt a little less alone.

Discussion Questions

1) God created you special and unique. How are you MORE than your disease?

2) Did the rhinoceros or zebra cause you to remember a painful shot or long hospital stay? Share what you felt while you were reading.

3) Cold waiting rooms and MRIs are no fun, but the medicine and care your doctors and nurses give you help you climb your mountains. Name a favorite doctor or nurse you have and how your medicine helps you do fun things—like going to the zoo and seeing all the cool animals that are in this book.

4)   If you're afraid to get a shot, stay in the hospital a long time, or hear kids say mean things to you, this is okay, but don't ever let fear keep you from climbing your mountains. Name some things you can do to be MORE than your fear.

5)   Has your disease ever made you feel you aren't enough? How can you show the world you're a bright shooting star?

About the Author

In 2013, WHITNEY was diagnosed with a rare gene mutation. In fact, it was so rare that she was the first person to have ever been diagnosed with the disease and the mutation was so horrific that she should not have survived her mother's pregnancy. After years of research on this new disease, Whitney was invited to give the new phenomenon a name. She chose to call it "MAGIS Syndrome." "MAGIS" is the Latin word for "more." She hoped the meaning would give future patients who are diagnosed with MAGIS Syndrome the assurance that they are MORE than their disease. Whitney hopes through her story, people of all ages will know despite the mountains they face, they are MORE!

About the Illustrator

COURTNEY SMITH grew up in southwestern Colorado and attended college at Regis University where she met and married a handsome rocket scientist. Together, they have welcomed five children and live in Franktown, Colorado.

Courtney raises Great Pyrenees puppies, teaches CPR, travels internationally with USA Olympic wrestling hopefuls as an athletic trainer, and cheers on her children. In her free time, she loves to draw and sketch, creating images to enhance incredible stories.

www.ingramcontent.com/pod-product-compliance
Lightning Source LLC
LaVergne TN
LVHW070800250326
834741LV00014B/144